WRESTLING
Contending on the Mat

PREPARING FOR GAME DAY

BASEBALL & SOFTBALL: SUCCESS ON THE DIAMOND

BASKETBALL: STRATEGY ON THE HARDWOOD

CHEERLEADING: TECHNIQUES FOR PERFORMING

EXTREME SPORTS: POINTERS FOR PUSHING THE LIMITS

FOOTBALL: TOUGHNESS ON THE GRIDIRON

LACROSSE: FACING OFF ON THE FIELD

SOCCER: BREAKING AWAY ON THE PITCH

TRACK & FIELD: CONDITIONING FOR GREATNESS

VOLLEYBALL: APPROACHING THE NET

WRESTLING: CONTENDING ON THE MAT

WRESTLING
Contending on the Mat

Peter Douglas

MASON CREST

Mason Crest
450 Parkway Drive, Suite D
Broomall, Pennsylvania 19008
(866) MCP-BOOK (toll free)

9 8 7 6 5 4 3 2 1

ISBN (hardback) 978-1-4222-3922-3
ISBN (series) 978-1-4222-3912-4
ISBN (ebook) 978-1-4222-7877-2

Cataloging-in-Publication Data on file with the Library of Congress

QR CODES AND LINKS TO THIRD-PARTY CONTENT

CONTENTS

KEY ICONS TO LOOK FOR:

Words to understand: These words with their easy-to-understand definitions will increase the reader's understanding of the text while building vocabulary skills.

Sidebars: This boxed material within the main text allows readers to build knowledge, gain insights, explore possibilities, and broaden their perspectives by weaving together additional information to provide realistic and holistic perspectives.

Educational Videos: Readers can view videos by scanning our QR codes, providing them with additional educational content to supplement the text. Examples include news coverage, moments in history, speeches, iconic sports moments and much more!

Text-dependent questions: These questions send the reader back to the text for more careful attention to the evidence presented there.

Research projects: Readers are pointed toward areas of further inquiry connected to each chapter. Suggestions are provided for projects that encourage deeper research and analysis.

Series glossary of key terms: This back-of-the book glossary contains terminology used throughout this series. Words found here increase the reader's ability to read and comprehend higher-level books and articles in this field.

 WORDS TO UNDERSTAND:

dynamic: marked by usually continuous and productive activity or change

expunged: having removed (something) completely

rejuvenated: restored to an original or new state

Chapter 1

MEET DAY

In the sport of wrestling, there is no one else to rely on. There is no one else out there on the mat with an athlete to pick you up when you make a mistake. There is no opportunity to substitute out of the match for a few minutes to rest, collect yourself, or refocus. Teammates can only offer encouragement from the sidelines. On the mat, facing the opponent, it is just athlete versus athlete and nothing else. That is why when the day of the meet arrives, wrestlers need to be well prepared.

"I don't want to hang on to win a match by one point. The sport needs guys that are going out there to score points."

– David Taylor, two-time NCAA national champion and College Wrestler of the Year

SLEEP

Being well rested is critically important to the performance of an athlete. There are studies that show that getting even two hours less than the optimal amount of sleep can affect performance on an equivalent level to having a 0.05 blood alcohol level. Sleep is not only key in making sure the body has energy to perform well at the next day's meet, but sleep also helps the body recover from the stresses of that day's meet.

What is the optimal amount of sleep? While there are ranges and some people do better on more or less sleep than others, experts

"Gold medals aren't really made of gold. They're made of sweat, determination, and a hard-to-find alloy called guts."

– Dan Gable, Olympic gold medalist

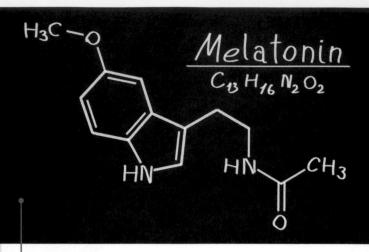

H₃C—O

Melatonin
$C_{13} H_{16} N_2 O_2$

HN

HN   CH₃

O

A dark sleep environment is necessary for the body to release the sleep-inducing chemical melatonin.

tend to agree that seven and a half to eight hours of sleep is the optimal amount the night before a meet.

Once a wrestler has set aside the correct amount of time for sleeping, the quality of that sleep should be maximized. There are a number of factors to consider in this regard: mattress, light, temperature, and noise.

First and foremost, the sleeping surface needs to be a good one. A low-quality or worn-out mattress can make it difficult to get a comfortable, uninterrupted night's rest. Sleeping on a substandard mattress can result in waking up with lower back pain or not being comfortable enough to fall into a deep sleep, which prevents the restorative effects of sleep from being maximized.

One of the chemicals released by the body to help it sleep is melatonin. The body only releases melatonin in low-light environments, which is why sleeping in a room with limited amounts of light is key to a good night's sleep.

It is also important for the room to be set at a good temperature. A warm room is not conducive to sleeping. The body's temperature follows its circadian rhythm, a built-in twenty-four-hour cycle tied to environmental cues. As night falls, so does the body's temperature, reaching a minimum shortly after falling asleep. In a warm room, the body cannot lose its heat, and it will be difficult to sleep well.

Noisy environments are obviously not desirable when trying to fall and stay asleep. If some external noise factors cannot be controlled, introducing a steady background noise into the sleep environment, such as a fan or white noise machine, can help to counteract those external elements.

NUTRITION

A rested body needs the proper fuel to help it perform well. Wrestlers also need to be stricter with their eating habits as maintaining a certain weight is vital. It is a balancing act to provide enough energy without storing any excess amounts.

As with most other high-activity sports, carbohydrate-rich foods give the muscles the energy they need for a tough match. A pre-meet meal should have a healthy serving of foods from grains (bread, cereal, rice, corn, and pasta) and fruits and vegetables.

"I train every day of my life as they have never trained a day in theirs."

– Aleksandr Karelin, nine-time world champion and three-time Olympic gold medalist

Protein is another significant element to include in a tournament-day meal. The National Wrestling Coaches Association (NWCA) recommends that about 20 percent of a wrestler's calories should come from protein. The rough rule of thumb is half a gram of protein per day for each pound of body weight. For example, a 150 lb. wrestler should eat at least seventy-five grams of protein on meet day. Good sources include lean meat like poultry or fish, beans, eggs and dairy such as cheese, milk, and yogurt.

Ideally, these carbohydrates, proteins, and all other nutrients should come from food and drink. It should not be necessary for wrestlers to take additional dietary supplements, with the possible exception of a multivitamin.

Wrestlers have unique circumstances when it comes to nutrition due to the need to maintain a strict weight. After they weigh in, the NWCA recommends concentrating on drinking lots of fluids before competing. An hour before the first match, wrestlers should drink two cups of a sports drink with sodium

Complex carbohydrates should make up a significant part of a pre-match meal.

Check out Olympic champion Helen Maroulis's healthy weight loss regimen.

and potassium, followed by another two cups of water fifteen to twenty minutes before the match. The sports drink should be low in carbs and sugar, with no more than sixty calories in eight ounces.

Wrestlers typically compete under a tournament format, meaning they will wrestle periodically throughout the day. The most important thing is for the athlete to maintain hydration consistently over this time. The NWCA also recommends snacking after each match, focusing primarily on carbohydrates with some protein. Milk, carrots, celery, fruit, cereal, or granola bars and yogurt are all good options.

FLEXIBILITY

Tightness in the body will lead to a tight performance on the mat. Wrestlers need to maximize their flexibility before matches to maximize their chances of performing well. Stretching pre-match is the key to doing this. Wrestlers should work on stretching out their hamstrings, quads, glutes, hip flexors, groin, and calves. The upper body should not be neglected either.

Flexibility is as necessary to a wrestler as strength or agility. It gives wrestlers the ability to perform attacks from difficult positions. Most importantly, perhaps, flexibility helps prevent injuries that might occur when the body is turned or twisted awkwardly, which frequently happens in the sport.

> "A wrestler should never restrict their water to the point where they are not able to consume water every day."
>
> – Leroy (Lee) Kemp, three-time world and NCAA champion

Wrestling programs such as the one at Ohio State University, which has produced champions like Kyle Snyder and Logan Steiber in recent years, employ a number of different types of stretches, including **dynamic**, static, and proprioceptive neuromuscular facilitation (PNF).

Dynamic stretching actively works a muscle through its full range of motion. Static stretches are more traditional, holding a stretch in a single position for a given period of time. Both types are done pre-match.

PNF stretching is performed post match and involves three different forms of stretches: slow-reversal-hold, contract-relax, and hold-relax. All involve having one athlete stretching out another. For example, in a contract-relax stretch, one partner pushes on the back of the other as they stretch the hamstrings. The wrestler being stretched contracts the hamstring for a few seconds and then relaxes. The push from the partner allows for a deeper stretch of the muscle.

All stretches are designed to work the total body, which is the key to a successful stretching session.

WARM-UP

Athletes spend months and years training and practicing, getting their bodies ready to compete at a high level. It is important to follow through on all that hard work by treating the body right immediately before competing as well.

A world championship silver and bronze medalist for the United States at 63 kg, Campbell University head wrestling coach Cary Kolat believes that a proper warm-up is an often overlooked key to success, especially in the first round of a tournament. He has posted the following warm-up routine on his website, kolat.com:

Jog/Tumble 3 min.

Clearing Ties 2 min.

20-20-20 high-pace, quick motions (push-ups, sit-ups, or squats)

Finishing Shots 3 min. (opponent 70 percent fight)

> *"Warm-up properly and the first round of the event will work in your favor more times than not. Don't lose matches only because you did not warm up and get the burn out of your body the day of an event."*
>
> *– Cary Kolat, NCAA Division I wrestling coach and 2000 Olympian*

Jogging in place is a common element to start a wrestling warm-up.

20-20-20 high-pace, quick motions (push-ups, sit-ups, or squats)

Sprints 1:30 min. (sprint, bounce, sprint, bounce, etc.)

Escapes/Rev 2 min.

20-20-20 high-pace, quick motions (push-ups, sit-ups, or squats)

Escapes to Takedown 3 min.

Jog 1 min.

Hand Fight 3 min. (30 sec., bounce)

Sprints 1 min.

Live Wrestling 5 min. (feet don't stalemate more than 10 sec. keep moving)

10-10-10 High-pace, quick motions (push-ups, sit-ups, or squats)

Shadow wrestling 2 min. (1 min to 30 sec. break, lots of motion)

Stretching for two and a half minutes before beginning this routine would make it thirty minutes in total. Kolat recommends starting to warm up about forty-five minutes before the first match, and not to hold back. His experience is that exposing the body to fatigue will program it to respond and fight through it rather than quit.

CONCENTRATE

Perhaps the toughest part of match-day preparation is getting in the necessary mind-set to be successful. Nerves and anxiety need to be overcome or controlled. Negative thoughts must be **expunged**. A calm, confident space must be found. If this is not accomplished, all of the hard physical work preceding the match will be wasted.

Wrestlers employ a number of different techniques to accomplish these goals. Some develop the techniques on their own, while others learn them from coaches or books like *Mental Training for Peak Performance*, by Steven Ungerleider, PhD. The idea is to employ a device that uses a specific image to remove a negative thought, like putting the thought on a rocket and launching it into space, for example. Only positive thoughts are allowed to remain (i.e., "my technique is superior" or "my gut wrench cannot be stopped") along with positive imagery, such as scoring a takedown or executing an escape.

There are several sources of anxiety that wrestlers deal with before a match. Examples include the consequences of losing, non-wrestling distractions, fear of failure, expectations of others, and lack of confidence.

Some of this type of anxiety can be alleviated by managing expectations. Wrestlers must always expect to win—confidence is necessary. That victory, however, does not need to come from a pin or a technical superiority. A win is a win, and that should be the goal. Wrestlers should also focus only on the match at hand. Be confident of a victory but not so confident

"If I'm trying to prepare for a match, I'm trying to calm myself down. I like to listen to R&B. I like to listen to a little bit of slower paced stuff, so I won't get all hyped up. I won't have a lot of anxiety. I can just relax my heart rate and be relaxed."

– Jordan Burroughs, three-time world champion and Olympic gold medalist

" I don't think about losing. I think about winning every single time I step on the mat. I imagine myself wrestling the greatest wrestler of all time and beating him every single day. "

— Kyle Dake, 2013 College Wrestler of the Year

that you are looking past the current opponent to the next round of the tournament. Conversely, if the likelihood in the next round is to face an opponent who has bested you in the past, you will never get the chance for redemption if you do not win the match at hand. Stay in the present by preparing yourself to face one opponent at a time. Have confidence in the preparation and training you have done to get to the current match.

There will always be reasons for nerves and conditions that cause tension. A mentally prepared wrestler should expect and anticipate these situations and have solutions to deal with them.

> *"My high school coach told me 'A lion doesn't listen to music before he hunts,' so I typically just go out there and wrestle."*
>
> *– Kyle Snyder, world and Olympic champion*

Sports psychologists will often teach imagery as a technique for mental preparation, where athletes use their imaginations to simulate the sight, sound, and feeling of successful outcomes, like a throw or a pin. Teams will also employ mental professionals to teach their wrestlers relaxation techniques, like closing their eyes and imagining muscles becoming relaxed and heavy, then imagining walking on a beach or another calming environment. The object is to leave the athlete feeling relaxed and **rejuvenated**.

Whatever method ends up being effective for the individual wrestler is the one he or she should stick with. Routine is important, physically and mentally. Wrestlers must insulate themselves from distractions and get to that place that inspires them to succeed.

TEXT-DEPENDENT QUESTIONS:

1. For optimal sleep, should the temperature in the room be warm or cold?

2. What are the main reasons a wrestler should be flexible?

3. What are several sources of anxiety that wrestlers deal with before a match?

RESEARCH PROJECT:

Take some time, and put together a pre-meet routine for yourself. Be detailed in each element, outlining specific numbers of repetitions for warm-ups, and so on. Outline meals, rest, and all the necessary components that you feel could help best prepare you before a big meet.

WORDS TO UNDERSTAND:

execute: to carry out, accomplish

stamina: the ability or strength to keep doing something for a long time

tactic: a device for accomplishing an end

Chapter 2

THE RIGHT MINDSET

Wrestling is a combat sport. The extreme physical nature of hand-to-hand battles with opponents makes wrestling a sport that has a high incidence of injuries. More than half of American high school wrestlers will experience at least one injury during a season. This is not surprising given the nature of the sport. In wrestling, certain elements, such as particular holds and throws, involve inflicting pain upon the opponent. As a result, injuries should be expected. With the right mental approach, however, these can be minimized.

KNOW YOUR LIMITATIONS

One of the most important principles that successful wrestlers possess is self-control. Wrestlers must know which techniques they can use and which are beyond their skill level. They are not tempted to try something that is beyond their current abilities, therefore opening themselves to the possibility of being scored on or, worse, being injured. Dominating an opponent who is competing strongly to win a match requires fast, powerful, and skillful techniques rather than just brute force. Many young wrestlers want to apply advanced techniques well

Wrestlers must be honest about their skill level, knowing which moves they can execute and which are still beyond their capabilities.

before they are physically capable of executing them safely and skillfully. Sometimes wrestling books will advocate these techniques, so wrestlers need to be sure they are reading books targeted to their skill level. Unless they are written for beginners, wrestling books may contain a large number of advanced moves aimed at a more skilled and experienced audience. Do not attempt to apply these techniques without first running them past your coach. A difficult hip toss or double-leg takedown could strain your back muscles and result in injury if performed incorrectly.

Any training regimen should be designed by a coach to progress from the most basic of techniques to the most advanced. For competitions or sparring sessions, use only those techniques that have been well practiced and are familiar so that they come naturally. Progress with advanced techniques will be slow, but this is where self-control is again important. Focusing on what has been achieved in training rather than what is left to learn will help avoid frustration. Knowing a few basic techniques very well is superior to only being able to **execute** advanced techniques poorly.

BE DISCIPLINED

It may be tempting for wrestlers learning the sport to skip training sessions for what seem like very good reasons. A successful wrestler, however, has strong self-discipline. The sport requires strength, athleticism, and high levels of **stamina** and flexibility. Superior physical condition reduces the risk of injury. Attaining this kind of condition requires self-discipline; it means hours of physical training on top of the time spent practicing technique and maneuvers. Self-discipline does not come naturally to many people, but the rewards are often worthwhile.

Here are some ways to increase your self-

Virginia Cavalier Wrestling Club President Jim Harshaw talks about self-discipline.

discipline:

- Set realistic training goals and schedule specific days or times for completing them. By meeting each goal, you become more capable of setting higher standards for yourself.

- Do not lose sight of what you are trying to achieve. Everything that is worth achieving takes effort, and all the world's great wrestlers have had to go through exactly the same process of development. Picture your own goal—such as being a local or state champion—before, during, and after every training session.

- Reward yourself every time you meet one of your training goals. Perhaps there is something special you want to buy or take a training session off to do something special instead.

- Remember that the ability to work hard is a gift, and the work should not be seen as a chore—without hard work, your dreams will remain only dreams.

Self-discipline helps wrestlers stick to their training regimens, which will improve fitness levels and therefore enhance their abilities to master tougher techniques. Wrestlers should be honest about their capabilities, however. Wrestling well requires confidence, but overconfidence can lead to unwanted results. Pushing beyond your capabilities will result in injury and discouragement. Capabilities can be expanded through practice and training, but athletes need to be realistic about how they are progressing. Athletes progress at different rates. Just because a teammate can execute certain skills does not mean that you necessarily can. Have the self-discipline to be patient. It is also important to prepare correctly for training sessions. When you are tired, hungry, or feeling sick, your body cannot perform optimally or even adequately. You might be tempted to push yourself during these times, but doing so will only expose you to injury or further illness as your body attempts to perform in its weakened state.

DEVELOP TOUGHNESS

Like any contact sport, wrestling can sometimes involve situations that cause physical pain. Wrestlers will be more successful if they can develop a high pain threshold. It may sound counterintuitive at first, but the ability to tolerate more pain is actually likely to lead to fewer rather than more injuries. Wrestlers with a low pain threshold are apt to try to avoid or try to stop pain, which is likely to induce decisions that lead to mistakes, which in turn leads to greater exposure to potential injury.

Learning to be tough in the face of physical pain is not fun. Raising your pain threshold begins by experiencing pain itself. Whenever you experience pain during a wrestling match, tell yourself mentally that you can handle it and that you are not going to quit. Of course, you are right to submit if the pain is excruciating, but if you feel that you can

Learning to be tough when facing physical pain is essential for wrestling success.

endure it, then hang on, and try to find a way out of the situation. That is the kind of toughness wrestlers need to possess to be successful. Practice thinking positively, and keep thinking clearly about how you can escape or fight back. Focus all your energy on winning the bout rather than simply surviving it. A winning attitude is tough and resilient; any weakness will be found by your opponent and mercilessly exploited. Having a strong mind will also make your body produce its optimum performance and so provide the strength to resist attacks that might produce injury.

EQUIPMENT

Wrestlers wear little in the way of protective clothing in competition. In training and in collegiate wrestling, however, there are more options available.

Perhaps the most vulnerable extremity on a wrestler is the ears. During sparring, ears can be torn, crushed, or bruised due to headlocks, accidental head butts, or impact from assorted other body parts. Years ago, many seasoned wrestlers had characteristic "cauliflower" ears, which were misshapen and resembled the vegetable due to the way they were deformed after healing from damaging blows. A popular piece of modern safety equipment is a set of ear guards. These protect against the blunt force impact that causes this damage. Worn over the head, a set of ear guards consists of a fabric sling containing two foam ear pads that fit snugly to the side of the head. These will protect the ears during even the hardest clashes and prevent tearing, but make sure that your coach helps you fit the guards properly before you spar. Ear guards are an inexpensive way to get effective protection.

Another vulnerable area for wrestlers whose heads often come together during sparring is the mouth. A clash between the top of your opponent's head and your mouth is likely to damage your teeth. This is why many wrestlers wear a mouth guard. This piece of equipment is designed to protect the vulnerable top row of teeth. Mouth guards are most definitely a good idea as they reduce the chance of losing teeth if the opponent's elbow or head hits your mouth or if you strike your mouth on the floor during sparring. The most basic mouth guard is one you fit yourself. This is a jaw-shaped piece of plastic that softens when placed in boiling water.

You then put the softened mouth guard onto your top set of teeth and suck it hard so that it molds itself to the shape of your teeth. Once it cools, it will retain a personal fit to your mouth. When fitting a mouth guard, always be careful to drain it to avoid burning your mouth on any boiling water that is trapped in the guard.

Custom mouth guards are also available and are commonly available from most dentists. A cast is taken of your mouth, and a mouth guard is then made to this model. The mouth guard will be fitted properly so that it is exactly contoured around every tooth. A custom mouth guard can even be fitted for a fixed brace. There are also mouth guards that protect both the top and bottom sets of teeth. These are fitted with ventilation holes so that breathing is not affected, but many athletes prefer not to wear these more cumbersome guards.

BASIC OUTFIT

The typical wrestling uniform consists of a one-piece uniform called a singlet. These are usually made of nylon, Lycra, or a similar flexible material.

Wrestlers wear special equipment, including shoes with high ankle support.

They are designed to avoid constricting material around the shoulders or arms as you need to be able to move as freely as possible during matches.

Singlets should be washed after every practice or match due to the heavy amount of sweating that takes place, both from the wrestler and the opponent. Sweat buildup in the singlet can lead to bacteria growth and, in turn, skin problems. Unless you do laundry every day, it would be most efficient to have at least three singlets during wrestling season.

Knee protectors are another valuable piece of wrestling equipment. The twisting and grappling actions associated with wrestling can be tough on an athlete's knees, and knee issues are common among wrestlers. Knee protectors hold the kneecap, or patella, in place, and help stabilize the ligaments of the joint. This helps protect the knee from injury during pushing or twisting actions. The stability also disperses the force of blows to your knee away from your kneecap, lessening any damage. Good knee protectors are made from thick neoprene, an elasticized material with excellent supportive and protective properties. The basic knee protector is a neoprene sheath that is worn around the knee.

Last but certainly not least is footwear. Wrestling shoes are a key component of a wrestler's equipment. Proper wrestling shoes are designed for the specific movements of the sport, as opposed to more general training shoes. Wrestling shoes have several features that help prevent injury to the feet and ankles: They have high ankle support to grip the ankle and make it less vulnerable to twisting and sprains. The sole of the shoe will often have a split design so that the shoe can cope with the flexing demands placed on it when the wrestler is pushing or squatting.

WRESTLING MATS

Wrestlers do not often have control over the type of wrestling mat they end up practicing or contesting matches on. There are, however, some key things to be aware of with this equipment.

- Make sure that there are no gaps between the mats. Gaps can result in sprained ankles if feet slip into them. Point out this problem as soon as you notice it. Mat tape can be used to secure the mats to one another and also make repairs of any tears in the fabric.

- Clean up any sweat or water from mats between sparring to prevent slipping.

- At the end of the day, the mats should be cleaned with proper antifungal and antibacterial mat cleaner to stop the transference of skin problems among athletes. The underside of the mats should be cleaned at least once a week.

- If you have to clean up blood, wear rubber gloves. First, soak up the blood with paper towels, and then clean the area with disinfectant.

SIDEBAR
Cauliflower Anyone?

In the United States, it is mandatory for wrestlers to wear ear protectors both in practice and during matches. These consist of a set of straps that fasten with either snaps or Velcro with hard, plastic-covered foam protectors attached. In wrestling, the ears of the athlete are subject to frequent impact from the opponent's head, and this battering often crushes blood vessels within the ear to block the flow of blood. The cartilage that shapes the ear is then unable to receive nutrients and dies. The blocked blood pools in the ear, and scar tissue forms, giving the ear a bumpy, deformed shape resembling a cauliflower. Treating the injury by draining the blood from the ear and using stitches to reconnect tissue before applying a pressure dressing can prevent cauliflower ear. The most effective prevention, however, is to invest in a custom measured set of ear protectors from a reputable manufacturer that your coach can likely recommend.

IMAGERY

The use of imagery as a mental preparation **tactic** is now common in many sports and is an effective tool for wrestlers. Basically, imagery is the practice of using your imagination as a mental training tool to develop confidence.

Getting a pin is a scene that a wrestler using the mental preparation technique known as imagery might imagine.

Researchers have discovered that athletes who spend time imagining themselves doing well at their sport actually improve more quickly than those who concentrate only on physical development. They are also better at acquiring new skills. Imagery uses not only visualization but also expands to imagining the sounds and tactile elements of success as well. Imagery also helps prevent injuries by improving technique. For wrestling, here is an example of how imagery is used:

- Find a quiet place, away from other people, where you can sit still or lie down. Close your eyes.

- Relax your body by focusing on the ebb and flow of your breathing. At the same time, imagine each muscle of your body softening like butter on a warm windowsill, working from your toes to your scalp.

- Imagine performing a technique that you are currently learning. Even if you cannot perform the technique yet, imagine yourself doing it perfectly, throwing, taking down, or pinning your opponent with total confidence. Mentally rehearse the technique again and again; imagine yourself doing it perfectly, throwing, taking down, or pinning your opponent with total confidence. Mentally rehearse the technique time and time again, starting off slowly and then building up speed and power.

- The key to imagery is imagining everything in detail: sights, sounds, and how things feel. See the picture in color, and notice details about your surroundings, such as noise, items of equipment, the appearance of your opponent, and so on. A clear picture will make the mental training more realistic.

- Once you have rehearsed the technique in your imagination, take three deep breaths. On the third breath, open your eyes.

TEXT-DEPENDENT QUESTIONS:

1. The sport requires strength, athleticism, and high levels of what?

2. Raising your pain threshold begins by experiencing what?

3. What does the typical wrestling uniform consist of?

RESEARCH PROJECT:

Look into how much it will cost to assemble a complete complement of wrestling equipment, including singlets, headgear, knee protectors, mouth guards, and shoes. Set a realistic budget for yourself, and examine what sacrifices in equipment you need to make to put together the best possible set.

 WORDS TO UNDERSTAND:

elasticity: the capability of a strained body to recover its size and shape after deformation

sap: to gradually diminish the supply or intensity of something

susceptible: capable of submitting to an action, process, or operation

Chapter 3

TRAIN FOR SUCCESS

Wrestling is one of the most physically demanding of sports. It places tough demands upon an athlete's strength, endurance, and flexibility. Inexperienced wrestlers will too often concentrate only on developing their strength while neglecting their endurance and flexibility, which exposes them to injury.

Wrestlers are **susceptible** to two main types of injury. The first type is impact injuries, which happen when wrestlers' bodies collide or when wrestlers take a hard fall on the mat. Causes of impact injuries include head butts (which constitute about 30 percent of all wrestling injuries), getting poked in the eye, taking an elbow in the face, and hard throws onto the back, hip, or shoulder.

The impacts, twisting, and wrenching that occur in wrestling make injury a real possibility.

The second type is twisting or wrenching injuries. Many wrestling techniques are aimed at bending body joints against the natural limits of their movement to inflict pain while establishing control of the opponent. Alternatively, they may be designed to throw the opponent with sudden explosive movements. Both types of techniques can result in a variety of injuries. These include strains, dislocations, torn ligaments or muscles, and even fractures. Injuries are much more likely to occur in athletes who have poor flexibility or weak muscle tone.

SIDEBAR

Overtraining

In the United States, about 3.5 million kids under age fourteen are treated for sports-related injuries each year. Of these, roughly half of them are overuse injuries such as rotator cuff tears, tendinitis, or shin splints. In the vast majority of these cases, the fault behind the injuries lies not with the kids but rather with the adults in their lives. Parents tend to overlook warning signs of overwork, such as general exhaustion and fatigue, mood swings, weight loss, and loss of interest. Coaches have a "no pain, no gain" mentality when what these kids really need in many instances is rest. Young wrestlers need time for their bodies to heal in between workouts or practices.

"The frequency and duration of practices could be limited, and coaches and parents could educate children making them aware of the potential for overuse injury," said Matt Brzycki, assistant director of campus recreation and fitness at Princeton University.

The tougher the practice, the longer the athlete will need to recover. Coaches need to be more aware of the capabilities of individual athletes,

and parents need to recognize the signs of potential overuse issues in their kids before injuries happen. As a wrestler, if you are feeling tired or sore, let a coach or parent know. Taking it easy for a practice or two is a much better alternative than a trip to the doctor.

FLEXIBILITY TRAINING

Flexibility gives muscles and ligaments greater elasticity, and this makes them less likely to experience strains or tears when put through extreme ranges of movement. Flexible wrestlers are therefore much more likely to withstand injuries. For wrestlers, the most vulnerable areas in terms of strain are the back, neck, shoulders, hips, knees, and ankles. A wrestler's flexibility training should aim to increase the flexibility of these areas to their maximum extent. When you warm up for sparring, use stretches that specifically target these areas, and use them in dedicated stretching sessions at least three times a week. The following are just a few examples of effective techniques to increase flexibility.

NECK STRETCH

Stand upright, facing forward. Pull your chin down to your chest, and hold for a couple of seconds. Then rock your head backward and look up at the ceiling, stretching the neck upward while you do so. Repeat this set of stretches three times. Then twist your head to the left and right (five times on each side), stretching the neck to the fullest extent. Finally, rotate your head in large circles, remembering to pull your head up rather than back at the top of each circle.

HIP STRETCH

Stand upright with your legs in a wide A shape about two shoulder-widths apart. Bend forward from the waist, and put your body weight on your hands. Now slowly sink your hips downward, inching your legs wider and wider apart. Keep breathing deeply as you do this, and go down only as far as you can manage. When you are at your limit, hold the position for five to ten seconds, and try to relax your muscles. You may find that you can go down a little farther after doing this. When you have reached your maximum stretch, come out of the stretch by walking your feet inward (while maintaining your weight on your hands) until you are able to stand up.

LEG STRETCH

Sit on the floor with both legs straight out in front of you. Draw one leg in so that the sole of the foot sits against the inner thigh of the extended leg. Sit up straight and breathe in deeply, then exhale slowly and bend forward from the hips and waist over your extended leg until you can grip your foot. Slowly pull on the toes so that the heel lifts slightly off the floor. You should feel a deep stretch along the back of the leg and knee. Finally, lower the heel to the floor, and sit up.

BACK STRETCH

Lie on your back. Bend your knees, and draw your legs up so that your feet are flat on the floor near your buttocks. Place your hands on either side of your neck with your fingers under the shoulders, pointing down your body. Breathe in, then push with your feet and hands and raise your abdomen toward the ceiling. You should end up in an arched shape, a stretch usually known as "a bridge." Be careful not to put any weight on your head—doing this makes you run the risk of a neck injury. Hold the stretch for a few seconds, and then lower yourself back down to the starting position. Repeat two more times. If you do not have the power to lift yourself up, have a partner support your inner back throughout this stretch. This stretch is ideal for developing the "bridge" position used to resist a fall.

ANKLE STRETCH

While sitting down with the legs outstretched, put the left ankle on top of the right knee. Hold the raised ankle with your left hand, and take hold of the toes and the ball of the foot with your right hand. Using your right hand, circle the foot around in one direction in large circles, repeating ten times

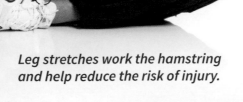

Leg stretches work the hamstring and help reduce the risk of injury.

before turning it in the opposite direction. Then pull your foot up, stretching it toward your shin. Hold the stretch and breathe out. Finally, pull the foot in a stretch away from the shin. Repeat for the other foot.

STRETCHING RULES

Whatever stretch you are doing, obey these important rules to have a safe and effective session:

- Stop if you experience any sharp or burning pains.

- Do not attempt to rush flexibility—stretching too hard will just result in an injury.

- Do not bounce yourself deeper into the stretch. Jerking movements increase the possibility of muscle or ligament injury.

- Practice flexibility training regularly, at least every other day. You will soon notice a genuine improvement in your flexibility.

- Always warm up before stretching. Do some light exercise, such as fast walking or very light running, to raise your body temperature. Circle your hips, and swing your arms to loosen the major joints and shake out any stiffness. Warm muscles respond much better to stretching than cold muscles and are less likely to be injured.

- Do not stretch a limb or area that is suffering from an injury.

Your coach should give you a flexibility program custom-made to your physical needs. If you have any questions, do not hesitate to ask your coaches.

ENDURANCE TRAINING

Wrestling requires a high level of fitness, and endurance is an important element of fitness in the sport. A loss of endurance will **sap** a wrestler's strength late in matches. When they tire and become weak, wrestlers will also be vulnerable to injury. Many injuries occur when people weaken through fatigue, and this is far more likely to happen in an unfit athlete.

Endurance can be built up in a number of ways. One of the most common and effective methods is through regular aerobic exercises. Aerobic exercises are those that raise the heart rate and breathing, requiring more oxygen throughout the body to fuel the effort. Typical examples include running, cycling, and swimming. Try to incorporate all three in your training regime.

The most tried and true aerobic exercise is running, which is probably the best overall method for increasing endurance. Try to run three times a week. If you are new to running, maintain a light pace for about twenty to thirty minutes. As you become more fit, increase the length of time that you run. Set your runs in time, not distance. If you measure in distance, the tendency will be to exercise for shorter periods of time as you become fitter. Instead, work on trying to run a greater distance in the same time as your last run. During your long-distance run, insert thirty-second bursts of speed running. The speed runs train your heart and respiration to reach maximum output while already working hard. Also, practice short sprints of 100 to 200 yards (about 90 to 180 m) with rest periods in between. Your basic aim while running is to raise your heartbeat to around 150 beats per minute and to keep it there for at least fifteen minutes. You can buy a simple electronic wristband that displays your heart rate while running. Be sure to invest in good running shoes that provide plenty of ankle support and grip, and alternate between running on road surfaces and soft surfaces, such as grass and earth. These measures will help guard against conditions such as shin splints, stress fractures, and muscle strains.

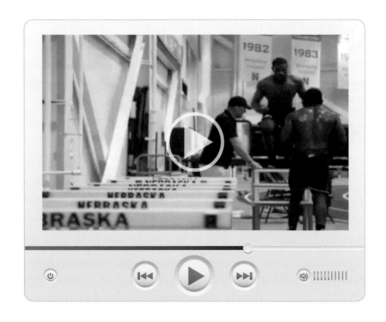

Check out world and Olympic champion Jordan Burroughs's intense training routine.

Endurance training increases cardiovascular fitness and allows wrestlers to tire more slowly.

STRENGTH TRAINING

The aim here is not to stress the importance of flexibility and endurance over strength in the sport of wrestling but rather to point out that all three are equally necessary for success. Strength training is essential for a wrestler. Not only does it help you competitively, but it also guards you against injury. Strong muscles are less likely to be strained or torn than weak ones, and they also help prevent dislocations of the joints by holding the joint firmly in place.

Weightlifting is a traditional method of strength training. The resistance muscles overcome by repeatedly lifting heavy objects makes them stronger. Strength training can also be done without weights by using age-old techniques such as push-ups, crunches, and lunges. For stomach conditioning, use crunches rather than traditional sit-ups. During crunches, you curl your body up off the floor but keep the small of your back on the floor. This is healthier for you than sit-ups as research indicates that sit-ups place too much strain on the lower spine and back muscles.

For a more focused approach to strength training, working with weights is a more scientific method of isolating individual muscle groups. Use free weights in particular rather than weight machines. Free weights train your balance as well as build up your muscular strength. Your coach should be able to explain a full program of weight training to develop your strength, as long as it is appropriate for your development. Young teen athletes can do damage to their bodies if they use weights before their bodies are ready. Here we can look at some general principles of strength training to help protect your body from injury:

- Weight training should be done regularly, especially in season. Wrestlers often concentrate on strength training during the off-season, when they are able to give more time to the discipline. The important point is that the training is regular and disciplined. The ideal is about seventy-five minutes, three times a week, varying routines to work different muscle groups. You can train more than that, but leave at least three days of the week for rest so that your body can recover.

- During the weight-training session, it is vital that you exercise pairs of muscles rather than single muscles. For example, on the inside of the upper arm are the biceps and on the outside are the triceps, which are more likely to be injured. Giving equal attention to both biceps and triceps produces a stable muscle system in the arm.

Working muscle groups in pairs is vital throughout the body. Opposing muscle groups are known technically as antagonistic muscle groups, and there are four main ones that require exercising: chest and laterals; biceps and triceps; abdominals and lower back muscles; and quadriceps and hamstrings. Be particularly careful not to develop your abdominal muscles at the expense of your back muscles. Strong abdominal muscles may be attractive to look at, but you will quickly forget this if you happen to pull your back in a wrestling match.

Ideally, weight training should take place under the supervision of an experienced trainer, someone who knows how to develop a program to maximize results while minimizing the chance of injury. What is most important is to learn good technique; performing exercises poorly can lead to injury. Increase the loads you lift very gradually, building up your strength slowly rather than attempting to push too far ahead. Remember, being muscular will not in itself win a wrestling match. Only technique can do that.

Wrestling is a sport that strikes a balance between body bending flexibility, explosive strength, and arduous feats of endurance. By paying attention to all aspects of your fitness, your body will be far better able to resist both sudden and gradual injuries. But injuries will still occur sometimes—so it's important to know how to handle them.

Leg presses can help give a wrestler the strong base he or she needs to succeed.

Doing crunches is an effective exercise for strengthening the core muscles of the body.

KEY MUSCLE GROUPS

- Leg muscles: It is important to have a strong base. There is no such thing as a successful wrestler with weak legs. Strengthen them by performing leg-press, leg-extension, and leg-curl exercises on weight machines. Alternatively, hold a pair of dumbbells down by your sides and practice lunges: step forward deeply with one leg, then step back, alternating between legs.

- Neck muscles: Some gyms will have weight machines specifically designed to strengthen the neck muscles on all four sides.

- Mid-section muscles: Applying twisting and turning techniques requires very strong abdominal and lower-back muscles. Engage in regular and oblique stomach crunches; these are like sit-ups but performed straight or to each side of the body without putting pressure on the spine. Alternatively, use the rotary torso machine found in most gyms.

- Hands and forearms: A simple pair of spring-loaded grip trainers is an effective tool to help develop strong finger, hand, wrist, and forearm muscles, which are vital for gripping and controlling an opponent.

TEXT-DEPENDENT QUESTIONS:

1. Wrestlers are susceptible to what two main types of injury?

2. Name three stretching rules.

3. What kind of training is essential for a wrestler?

RESEARCH PROJECT:

Take some time to do a routine to improve your flexibility, endurance, and strength. Which type of training do you enjoy most? Record detailed results, and indicate which area is the strongest and which needs the most improvement.

WORDS TO UNDERSTAND:

acute: characterized by sharpness or severity, having a sudden onset

hydration: the process of causing something to absorb water

trauma: a wound or shock produced by sudden physical injury, as from violence or an accident

Chapter 4

TAKING CARE OF THE BODY: INJURIES AND NUTRITION

Injuries are going to happen in wrestling. It is simply a function of the nature of the sport. No matter how well prepared wrestlers are, both mentally and physically, injuries are difficult to avoid despite all proper precautions. In this chapter, we will look at two common areas that wrestlers injure: the neck and the back.

NECK INJURIES

No part of the body is exposed to as much force in wrestling as the neck. Not surprisingly, it is one of the most easily injured body areas in the sport. Many neck injuries are the result of muscle **trauma**, or nerves being trapped, squeezed, or stretched during sparring. The typical symptoms of such injuries include the following:

- An intense pain or ache in the neck, aggravated by movement (Sometimes the pain is not sensed until the head is moved, at which point there is a burning or stinging pain in the neck. The pain may extend down through the shoulder and into the arm or may be confined to the neck area alone.)

- Sensations of numbness, tingling, or weakness in the arms or hands

- Pain that results in headaches and nausea

- Inability to sleep due to difficulty in getting the head into a comfortable position

- Neck muscles that spasm and limited mobility in the neck

In the best scenario, these symptoms last only a few minutes from the moment of injury before the pain dissolves and everything returns to

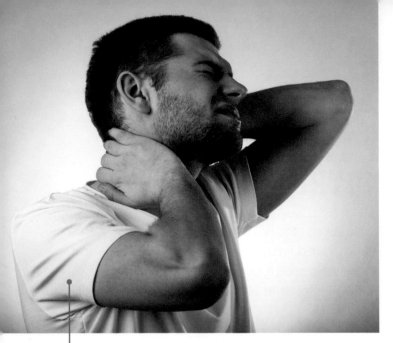

Sharp pain in the neck aggravated by head movement is a symptom of a neck strain, a common wrestling injury.

normal. If the pain persists, however, but is confined to the neck alone, take painkillers and apply heat or ice packs (whichever provides the best relief). Stop training, and give your neck plenty of rest. With such treatment, if the problem is a simple muscle strain, it should get better within a week.

Get professional help if the pain lasts longer, and do so earlier if the pain is radiating out into both arms or if you lost consciousness at the time of the injury. These symptoms can suggest serious injuries to the spine or an impairment of the spinal column, so a quick diagnosis is vital. If the problem is simply a pinched nerve, the physician will probably continue the treatment you are already doing or may give you a neck collar or recommend some physical therapy to relocate the nerves.

Ligaments, muscles, and bones of the neck may also be damaged at moments of hard impact. Simple neck sprains or strains have similar symptoms to pinched nerves. After the injury, apply ice packs to the injured area two or three times a day, for up to three days, to reduce swelling. Keep the ice packs on for no more than twenty minutes (any more and you run the risk of frostbite). Then apply heat ointments and anti-inflammatory medicines. Remember that a bad neck sprain can take more than a month to heal. Always visit a doctor for a proper diagnosis if the pain is particularly severe or if the injury is affecting the arms and shoulders.

Whiplash is a neck injury that requires immediate attention. This injury occurs when the neck is put through a traumatic flexing motion. There will be an immediate viselike pain in the neck, and the neck may become completely immobile. The pain of whiplash often extends up into the head and drives downward between the shoulder blades, out into the arms, and into the lower back. The injured person may experience nausea, dizziness, blurred vision, mood swings, and severe headaches. Without proper treatment, lifelong symptoms can result.

An ambulance should be called in severe cases of whiplash, and medical attention should always be sought. X-rays or other scans will produce an accurate diagnosis. Treatment varies according to severity. For minor whiplash, the doctor may fit a collar or recommend complete rest. However, doctors have recently begun to recommend letting the neck move, believing this to be a better route to recovery. Immobilization is now recommended only if pain cannot be well managed.

After about a week of complete rest, gently practice light exercises to loosen your neck, such as making small circles with the head or writing the alphabet in the air with your nose. For more severe whiplash, radical physical therapy and even surgery may be required. Follow your doctor's advice to the letter. Do not be tempted to return to wrestling until you are fully recovered with full, pain-free movement of the neck.

BACK INJURIES

Wrestling movements rely on sudden explosions of twisting, pushing, or lifting, motions that are all tough on the back and its muscles. Possible results include muscle strain or rupture in the back or even damage to the spinal column itself. Proper strength, flexibility training, and correct technique go a long way toward preventing back injuries. Yet backs often do become weaker as they wear down over the course of the wrestling season and are more prone to injury.

The symptoms of muscle strain or rupture in the back are fairly obvious. The athlete will experience severe pain in the back muscles, which will be made worse through movement or lifting. Mobility in the back and neck will be reduced. The best treatment is an initial period of complete rest. Controlling the pain is possible through painkillers and anti-inflammatory medication.

Light exercise to increase the back's flexibility and strength is recommended once the initial recovery from the pain occurs. For about a week, do gentle back stretches, such as standing side bends. Then perform light warm-up routines and the lightest of weight-training exercises with small weight loads.

Posture is important when recovering from back strains. The back should be kept straight with the shoulders drawn backward; imagine that you are being drawn up straight via a rope attached to the top of your head. Take hot baths to apply heat treatment to injured muscles.

A "slipped" or herniated disk is another common back injury in wrestling. A herniated disk can be caused by either degeneration or an **acute** injury. It results in the tissue of the spinal nucleus seeping out and pressing against the spinal cord and spinal nerves. The symptoms of a herniated disk are like those of other back problems yet can be even greater in their severity. Disk fluid can press upon the major nerve known as the sciatic nerve, resulting in shooting pain down the leg.

Consult a doctor right away if you begin to experience these symptoms. Lying on the floor with the legs bent at the knees over a chair can bring some relief, as the position pushes the small of the back onto the floor where it is supported, as will pain medication. Surgery may be required, however, if the injury is severe. The results of surgery are generally good, and the wrestler will usually be able to return to training after only six to ten weeks. If surgery is not chosen, you may have to wear a back brace to

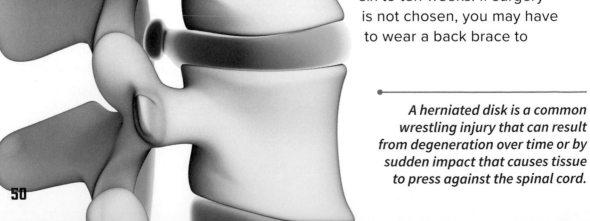

A herniated disk is a common wrestling injury that can result from degeneration over time or by sudden impact that causes tissue to press against the spinal cord.

Eating a healthy breakfast provides a wrestler's metabolism with a kick-start in the morning.

stabilize the injury while it heals, and apply hot or cold packs, according to your doctor's instructions. A trained physical therapist may apply massage or traction to aid healing.

NUTRITION

Your body can only be as good as what you put in it. The more balanced your diet is, the more you'll be able to stay fit and exercise at your full potential. Simply being mindful of what you take into your body will aid you in training for wrestling. Athletes need to consume a proper blend of nutrients to ensure that their bodies and minds are performing at their full potential.

Eating healthy foods is only one element of nutritional wellness. When you eat, how much, and whether you use dietary supplements are all factors that are just as important as what you eat. Before dramatically changing your diet or taking supplements, you should speak to your doctor about these changes. An athlete shouldn't make up his or her own nutritional program.

EATING TRAPS TO AVOID

The following are guidelines for what not to do when eating:

- Don't miss breakfast. Your body burns off extra fat slower without the kick-start in the morning which breakfast provides.

- Don't starve yourself while you exercise. Without food, the body will conserve fat even during exercise.

- Don't take a nap immediately after eating as this does not give your body the chance to burn off excess calories that you may have consumed.

- Don't eat your last meal late at night, and don't eat the most at your evening meal.

Try to follow how your body works best. Eat a generous breakfast and then a large lunch when you're active. Eat dinner early at night, and eat a light meal.

FOOD IN, ENERGY OUT

Wrestling is a sport where pounds matter. Like most athletes, wrestlers need to take in more than the 2,500 calories per day recommended for the average male. Although they do need more calories as fuel, wrestlers know that every calorie counts. This is a sport that classifies athletes by weight, measured down to the ounce. Therefore, wrestlers need to be mindful of their calorie intake.

Wrestlers must be vigilant about what they eat as they need to constantly monitor their weight.

#ForTheW

Check out the nutrition plan for wrestlers at Division I University of Wisconsin.

Wrestlers need to watch their calories because if they do not make weight at a meet, it means weeks of practice are wasted. Athletes should set a goal for weight class and always keep it in mind. That weight class goal, however, needs to be realistic. Weight class decisions should be part of the strategy worked out by the coach. If you are slightly above a weight division, then safely attempt to gradually drop your weight to fit that division. If you find yourself in the middle of a weight division, concentrate on maintaining the same weight while increasing muscle weight versus weight in fat.

Sometimes the decision as to what weight class to wrestle in comes down to simple math. The principle behind the formula for weight loss is simple: You want to burn more calories than you take

> " I eat big hearty meals three times a day. A lot of pasta, a lot of rice, spaghetti, gives us a lot of carbs and helps us stay energized for practice. "
>
> – Jordan Burroughs, three-time world champion and Olympic gold medalist

Wrestlers need carbohydrates but not the simple kind found in sugar. Unlike complex carbohydrates, sugar is high in calories and low in nutrients.

in. If you do this, you have a calorie deficit, and you lose weight. A deficit occurs when you lose more of something than you take in. So, if you want to lose two pounds (0.9 kg) of fat per week, which is a healthy goal (do not attempt more than this), you need to eat 100 calories less per day and burn 1,000 calories more per day.

WHAT TO EAT

CARBOHYDRATES

Carbohydrates have become the enemy of dieters and weight loss gurus in recent decades, but they are very necessary for athletes as they provide energy to the body. Between 50 to 65 percent of a wrestler's diet should be carbohydrates. Think of carbohydrates (also known simply as "carbs") as the fuel that you need to keep your body running through workouts and tournaments. There are two types of carbohydrates: simple and complex.

Sugar is the most commonly consumed form of simple carbohydrates. These break down faster and provide a burst of energy but bring your body down fast. Usually, they are full of empty calories, meaning the calorie content is high, but the food does not enrich the body. Americans know and love simple carbohydrate foods—candy, pop, and other sweets—but an athlete should avoid these. While athletes should avoid empty-calorie foods at all times, they should especially steer clear of these foods before workouts to avoid a "crash" or feeling of a lack of energy while they work out.

The far superior source of fuel comes from complex carbohydrates. These break down slower in the body and provide it with more nutrients. Vegetables, fruits, brown rice, whole-grain bread, beans, nuts, and cereal all contain complex carbohydrates. These complex carbohydrates give the body a longer-lasting boost of energy. Health professionals agree that switching from simple to complex carbohydrates is one of the smartest dietary choices a person can make. This can be as simple as buying whole-grain (brown) pasta instead of white, flour-based kinds at the supermarket. Most complex carbohydrate foods are good sources of fiber, which makes the body feel more full. This also helps weight loss by helping with appetite control.

PROTEIN
Proteins have become the darlings of the training world. They are important chemicals found in all living things that are used to perform functions inside our body's cells. Each protein is a long, folded chainlike molecule made up of "links" called amino acids. Our bodies break down proteins found in foods and build new proteins that give the body the building blocks needed to become strong. The best sources of proteins are meats and dairy products (like milk or cheese). Eggs and certain vegetables (such as soy beans) are an excellent source of protein as well. A good rule of thumb for how much protein to eat is that the number of grams should be equal to about one-third of your weight in pounds. For an athlete in training, it should be about one-half. For example, a 200-pound (90.7-kilogram) person should eat about 70 grams of protein every day. A 200-pound athlete should have 100 grams of proteins.

FATS
In excess, fats will clog arteries and lead to heart disease, but in the proper quantities, they help repair the body and can be used as sources of energy. Healthy skin, teeth, and hair require a steady diet of fat, as does healthy nerve function. Fatty foods should, however, make up no more than 25 percent of caloric intake. The kind of fat one consumes makes a difference as well; all fats are not created equal.

All fat is not bad for you, but wrestlers should avoid food with unhealthy trans fat.

There are three ways to classify fats: polyunsaturated, monounsaturated, and saturated. Unsaturated fat is good for the body, and saturated fats are best avoided. Monounsaturated fats (MUFA) are found in foods such as nuts, avocados, canola, and olive oil. These foods can help contribute to weight loss. Polyunsaturated fats such as salmon, fish oil, corn, and soy can help lower cholesterol. Omega 3 fatty acids are polyunsaturated fats found in fish oil. Fish oil can offer benefits such as healthier heart performance and cancer prevention. Omega 3 can even improve mental health.

Some popular protein sources, such as meat, dairy, eggs, and seafood all contain saturated fats, and too much of these are not healthy for your body. Oils such as coconut oil and palm oil also have "bad" saturated fat.

Scientists created so-called trans fats to preserve foods longer on the shelf. Many packaged foods like potato chips and microwavable popcorn contain trans fats. French fries from fast-food restaurants commonly have trans fats. The health effects of eating excessive trans fat are numerous and range from obesity and heart disease to infertility in women and even Alzheimer's, a degenerative neurological disease.

Eating saturated fats also leads to a sluggish feeling. Any kind of fat takes from three to five hours to fully digest, so it makes much more sense to stock up on complex carbohydrates for energy instead of fatty foods.

SIDEBAR
What to drink?

It will not come as a surprise to read that water is the recommended beverage to help athletes stay hydrated and should also be the beverage of choice in any situation. While the oft-cited recommendation that people should drink sixty-four ounces of water a day has been challenged for being misleading when applied to the general public (the Mayo Clinic says a variety of factors should be considered, including exercise level, health condition, temperature, and humidity of the environment), that guideline is about right for an athlete in training. People not in training will do just fine to drink when the body tells them it is thirsty. Both athletes and non-athletes, however, should stick primarily to water. More precisely, drinks with sugar or artificial sweeteners (these stimulate the release of hormones that slow your metabolism) should be avoided. In general, sugar-laden drinks provide empty calories and zero nutrition. Specifically for athletes, ingesting sugar after a workout affects insulin sensitivity and human growth hormone production. That so-called energy drink you like? Check the label. It likely contains significant sugar or artificial sweeteners. Energy is not what sweetened drinks ultimately provide. Any sugar rush quickly gives way to sluggishness as your pancreas works to balance out your blood sugar. What about electrolyte replacement, you ask? Experts say the processed sodium in sports drinks is a poor option for the job. It is a better idea to add a pinch of natural Himalayan salt to your regular water, which will replace eighty-four different minerals. If you don't have Himalayan salt handy, try some coconut water. It is available at almost any store that sells sports drinks and is one of the highest natural sources of electrolytes on the planet. The easiest and best course of action, however, is simple. Just drink some water.

WATER

The body's most essential nutrient does not contain any nutrients of its own. The body is made up of 60 percent water, and all parts of the body depend on water to function. Water is so important that the body can only go for about 72 hours without it, whereas it can survive for weeks without food.

Good **hydration** helps all parts of the body, including the brain. Water transports nutrients around the body and helps regulate temperature and metabolism. You should drink water before, during, and after exercise. Wrestlers in training should drink sixty-four ounces of water a day to replenish fluids. It is not necessary to drink that much on off-training days.

Hydration helps wrestlers to be healthier and prepare the body for optimum performance to gain muscle mass. Drinking water gives you more strength and endurance. Even a small amount of dehydration can decrease strength by 15 percent, so to maximize workout intensity, an athlete needs to be properly hydrated. The entire process of muscle gain is aided by water. Water also helps protect joints by assisting the body in joint lubrication.

Good hydration during training helps wrestlers maintain their strength and endurance.

TEXT-DEPENDENT QUESTIONS:

1. What part of the body is exposed to the most force in wrestling?

2. Name three traps to avoid when eating.

3. Healthy skin, teeth, and hair require a steady diet of what?

RESEARCH PROJECT:

Look up information on the artificial sweetener known as aspartame. What chemicals does it contain, and what do they do? What was aspartame originally created to do, and how is it used in the food supply today? Write a conclusion about your opinion of artificial sweeteners.

WORDS TO UNDERSTAND:

dominion: supreme authority

entrenched: established solidly

immortalized: having caused (someone or something) to be remembered forever

Chapter 5

WRESTLING: FROM ANCIENT GREECE TO AMERICA AND ADDING WOMEN

ANCIENT MAN TO MODERN AMERICA

Wrestling is perhaps the world's original sport. Prehistoric man drew pictures of themselves locked in one-on-one battles on cave walls up to 20,000 years ago. These ancient competitions may have determined clan leadership or who got the most food or the best shelter.

Wrestling is a natural test of strength that may have been used to simply settle disputes. Wrestling moves such as holds and throws have been discovered **immortalized** in art by ancient societies in every corner of the globe. One thing that these ancient depictions consistently demonstrate is that many of the moves shown are still used in the modern-day version of the sport.

In ancient Greece, citizens believed the gods of Olympus solved conflicts by wrestling with each other. One story tells of Cronus wrestling his son Zeus for possession of the universe, a match won by the son, making Zeus king of Olympia and giving him **dominion** over all. Another Greek hero, Theseus, is credited with creating the first rules of the sport. He grappled with and defeated the man with the bull's head known

Depictions of wrestling have been found in the art of ancient societies from all corners of the globe.

as the Minotaur. In the famous Greek saga the *Iliad*, written around 750 BC by Homer, Ajax and Odysseus wrestle each other during a feast. The match ends in a tie, and each wins a prize.

In 708 BC, wrestling is documented as a competition sport at the games of the eighteenth ancient Greek Olympiad. Although fundamentally the same as the modern sport, ancient Olympic wrestling had some unique differences to current versions. For example, the competitors were naked. They were also permitted to cover their skin with oil and sand, which made it difficult to hold them. There were two versions: upright, where the winner was the first wrestler to score three falls, and ground, where the athletes wrestled until one submitted, and all holds were permitted. Plato was a famous Greek philosopher, but Plato is not his actual

The famous Greek philosopher Plato was an Olympic wrestler as a young man.

name. Plato means "broad shoulders" in Greek. He earned the name due to his prowess as an Olympic wrestler as a young man, a fitting name for an athlete. His real name was Aristocles.

When the Romans took over the civilized world several centuries later, they ruled throughout what is now northern Africa and Europe, including Greece. The Romans adapted wrestling with their own modifications, and their version was far more violent than the one they learned from the Greeks, often ending in the death of one wrestler. The sport spread throughout the Roman Empire, gaining popularity in tribes from the Gauls to the Carthaginians.

Nearly 2,000 years later, knights and kings throughout Europe competed in wrestling matches. One of England's most famous kings, Henry VIII, was said to be a skilled wrestler, although legend has it that he once lost a match to Francis I of France.

The scene of this famous match was the Field of the Cloth of Gold in northern France. A three-week-long summit designed to improve French-English relations was underway in June of 1520. Wrestling competitions, along with archery displays and music, were among the entertainment. In a surprise move, Henry challenged Francis to the match but regretted it quickly as he lost in short order. The two countries were at war the next year.

Henry VIII, King of England, once lost a wrestling match to Francis I, King of France.

Organization and refinement grew within the sport as the centuries passed. In nineteenth-century France, a style developed where tripping and leg holds were not permitted. This style would eventually become what is known as modern-day Greco-Roman wrestling.

The ancient Greeks may have been history's most famous wrestlers, but the sport developed outside of Europe as well. This evolution came about in a very different way. The Japanese developed sumo wrestling, where two combatants meet inside a ring nearly fifteen feet (4.5 m) in diameter and attempt to push each other out of it or knock the opponent down. The first known sumo match took place in 23 BC, which according to legend was won by Sukune, the god of Japanese wrestlers. In the ninth century, the sons of the recently deceased emperor Buntoku wrestled

Sumo wrestling developed in Japan 2,000 years ago.

for the throne. An audience of thousands gathered to watch. About 300 years later, buke-zumo (warrior sumo) developed as part of the training for samurai.

The ancient cultures of the Americas also engaged in wrestling, just like their counterparts in Europe and Asia. From the Incas to the Iroquois, evidence of the sport of wrestling has been found among the original inhabitants of both North and South America. Native Americans wrestled in more of a free style, like the Romans. Matches were won by pinning the opponent's shoulders to the ground.

European settlers of the Americas also developed their own styles of wrestling, styles influenced by what they saw practiced by the people they conquered.

WRESTLING IN AMERICA

In America, freestyle wrestling has been the base of the sport since the mid-nineteenth century. This style allows for holds below the waist, unlike its Greco-Roman counterpart. Over the decades, however, it has evolved from the international variety to take on some distinctly American characteristics. Scholastic wrestling is the variation of freestyle wrestling practiced at the middle and high school levels in the United States. The National Federation of State High Schools Associations (NFHS) sanctions the sport in all states except Mississippi in fourteen weight classes.

Scholastic wrestling differs from freestyle in significant ways. Matches have three periods rather than two, with no breaks between periods. The first period begins in the neutral position. The wrestlers then take turns choosing the starting position for the second and third periods (assuming a fall does not end the match first). A technical superiority can also end the match if one wrestler accumulates a lead of fifteen points or more. Another difference of note is that wrestlers may only clasp

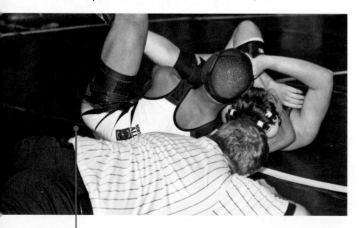

A move like this near fall is worth two to three points in collegiate wrestling.

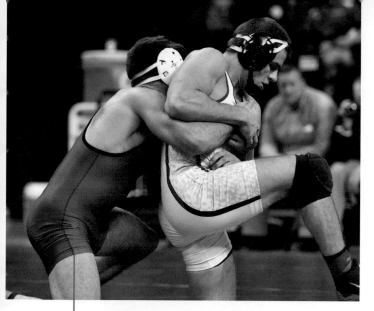

and lock their hands when attempting a takedown or pin. Unlike in freestyle, the move is considered illegal at any other time.

There are several ways to score in scholastic wrestling, such as exposing the opponent's back to the mat; holding the back to the mat but not long enough to score a pin (called a near fall and worth two or three points); escapes; reversals (worth two points rather than one in freestyle); and takedowns (worth two points whether by leg attack or by throw).

In collegiate wrestling, like this match between Harvard and Maryland, control is emphasized over explosiveness.

Overtime periods are held if the match is tied after regulation, starting with one minute of sudden death, then 2 thirty-second periods, and then if still necessary, a final thirty-second tiebreaker period. In scholastic wrestling, athletes are required to wear headgear to protect their ears.

The style of wrestling practiced at the college and university level in the United States is known as collegiate wrestling. This style, along with that of scholastic wrestling, is often collectively referred to as folkstyle wrestling, but there are differences between the scholastic and collegiate styles. The NCAA primarily sanctions the sport at the collegiate level but so too do the National Association of Intercollegiate Athletics (NAIA), the National Junior College Athletic Association (NJCAA), and the National Collegiate Wrestling Association (NCWA). There are ten weight classes for men and eight for women.

Yale and Columbia Universities held the very first intercollegiate meet in the United States in 1903. In 1927, an official set of rules was established for collegiate wrestling, and in 1928, the first NCAA wrestling championship was held at Iowa State. With its own set of rules firmly **entrenched**, this distinctly American brand of wrestling grew in popularity across the country.

This statue of wrestling legend Dan Gable stands at his alma mater, Iowa State University, where he won two NCAA titles as a wrestler and seventeen more as a coach.

The focus of collegiate wrestling is distinct from that of freestyle. In freestyle, elements of risk and explosiveness are highlighted over elements of control, which are more central to collegiate wrestling. Exercising control over the other wrestler and his or her movements is key to all styles of wrestling, but compared across styles, on levels of high risk to high control, there is less control in the freestyle discipline.

Throws are allowed in collegiate wrestling, for example, but are worth the same amount of points as any other takedown. In freestyle, throws are worth more. In collegiate wrestling, rather than picking opponents up, wrestlers try to break opponents down, getting them prone on the mat, where pinning techniques can be combined to achieve a fall.

America's homegrown folkstyle version has produced its share of stars who have not only succeeded at home but on the international freestyle stage as well.

America's legendary champions include John Smith, Dan Gable, Cael Sanderson, and Bruce Baumgartner.

On the national stage, none had the success of Gable and Sanderson. Gable came to prominence wrestling for his home state Iowa State University in the late 1960s. He dominated in his first varsity season, going 37–0. He went 30–0 the following year, including a stretch where he pinned a record twenty-five straight opponents at 137 lbs. (62 kg). In his senior year, he lost only the very last match of the season to finish as runner-up at 142 lbs. (64 kg).

Utah-born Cael Sanderson came to Iowa State thirty years after Gable starred there and continued the Cyclone tradition of wrestling excellence. He went unbeaten in his college career at 159–0, winning four straight NCAA titles and three Hodge trophies as the most outstanding college wrestler.

Both Gable and Sanderson each went on to win a single Olympic gold medal in freestyle, but on the international stage, Bruce Baumgartner was far more accomplished. Baumgartner, who grew up in New Jersey, had a good college career at Indiana State University, where he won a national championship, going 44–0 his senior year in 1982. Baumgartner went on to a stellar international career in the super-heavyweight freestyle division, winning four Olympic medals, including two gold, and nine world championship medals, including three gold.

John Smith is the greatest wrestler in American history and one of the greatest of all time from any country. He won back-to-back Olympic gold medals at 137 lbs. (62 kg) and four world championship gold medals, including three in a row.

KYLE SNYDER, WOMEN, AND THE OLYMPICS

Kyle Snyder of Woodbine, Maryland, is the current star of American freestyle wrestling. While a collegiate wrestler at Ohio State University, Snyder won both a 97 kg (214 lbs.) world championship and Pan Am Games gold medal in 2015 as well as an Olympic gold medal at the Rio Games in 2016. He is also a two-time NCAA Division I champion.

In men's freestyle, super heavyweight (125 kg)[276 lbs.] Taha Akgül of Turkey is a two-time world champion and the reigning Olympic champion.

At 86 kg (190 lbs.), Abdulrashid Sadulaev of Russia, like Akgül, has also won consecutive world championships in 2014 and 2015 and Olympic gold in 2016.

Russia's Roman Vlasov is a two-time Olympic gold medalist and two-time world champion in the Greco-Roman discipline.

On the Greco-Roman side is where wrestling's undisputed star plies his trade. Cuban giant Mijaín López, at 6'6", 290 lbs. (132 kg), is one of the best in the history of the sport. In Rio de Janeiro in 2016, López won his third consecutive Olympic gold medal in the super heavyweight class, now 130 kg. (286 lbs.) He has also won eight world championship medals, including five gold and three silver.

Other Greco-Roman stars include two-time world champion and 2016 Olympic gold medalist Artur Aleksanyan of Armenia at 216 lbs. (98 kg) and Roman Vlasov of Russia at 165 lbs. (75 kg). Vlasov has three world championship medals, including two gold, to go with consecutive Olympic gold medals, won in 2012 and 2016.

Watch American Kyle Snyder win the gold in Rio.

Women currently compete only in the freestyle category but have some incredible stars of their own. Chief among these is Japan's Kaori Icho. Icho, a legend at 128 lbs. (58 kg) for more than a decade, is a ten-time world champion. From 2003 to January of 2016, she won 189 straight matches. In a shocking result, Icho lost in a tournament in Russia to an unproven Mongolian opponent. She redeemed herself at the 2016 Olympics in Brazil by winning her unprecedented fourth straight gold medal.

Icho's teammate at 117–121 lbs. (53–55 kg), Saori Yoshida, is a thirteen-time world champion and, like Icho, won Olympic gold in 2004, 2008, and 2012.

SIDEBAR
Bear Slayer

America's best wrestlers understandably come out of the freestyle discipline, but arguably the most famous moment in American wrestling was distinctly Greco-Roman. At the 2000 Olympics in Sydney, Russian Aleksandr Karelin entered the competition as the clear favorite, having won three straight gold medals from 1988 through 1996 in the super heavyweight (130 kg [287 lbs.]) class, but that was the least of the accomplishments of the man called the Russian Bear.

Karelin had dominated the sport, coming into Sydney unbeaten for thirteen years and not having conceded a single point in six years. In the gold medal match, he faced American Rulon Gardner, a Wyoming farm boy who wrestled at the University of Nebraska. Karelin had beaten him 5–0 three years earlier in their only previous meeting. This time, Gardner fought off all his attacks and attempts to lift and throw him. His lone second-period point stood for the win and the historic upset, one of the biggest in any sport.

Ten-time world champion Kaori Icho of Japan, seen here being named the winner in a match in 2010, is the only wrestler to win four straight wrestling gold medals. She won her fourth in Rio in 2016.

Unlike Icho, however, Yoshida lost her bid for four consecutive Olympic gold medals when American Helen Maroulis beat her in Rio in 2016.

Maroulis grew up in Maryland and wrestled collegiately in Canada. Her upset of Yoshida gave the United States its first-ever gold in women's wrestling. Both Maroulis and Yoshida came into Rio as 2015 world champions, Maroulis at 121 lbs. (55 kg) and Yoshida at 117 lbs. (53 kg). At the Olympics, however,

The United States' Helen Maroulis, shown on the right in a 2013 match, won the Olympic gold medal at 121 lbs. (55 kg) at the Rio Olympics in stunning fashion over three-time defending champion Saori Yoshida of Japan. It was the first Olympic gold in women's wrestling in U.S. history.

the 55 kg class is not offered, forcing the two champions to compete for the same medal at 53 kg, and Maroulis prevailed.

It will be interesting to see what impact Maroulis's historic victory in Rio has on the sport in America. More than 11,000 girls were registered wrestlers at the time of her big Olympic moment, already more than ten times the number that wrestled twenty years earlier. Wrestling's governing body, United World Wrestling (UWW), reports that women's wrestling is its fastest-growing segment worldwide, with almost all 177 member nations sponsoring a woman's team. In 2016, the Olympic Games added two women's weight classes to the competition and removed two classes from the men's side. Therefore in 2016, Greco-Roman, men's freestyle, and women's freestyle each had six weight classes.

This gender equality is especially important at the Olympic level. Wrestling is under intense scrutiny to maintain its standing as a core Olympic event, which it has held since 1896. In 2013 the International Olympic Committee (IOC) voted to drop wresting from the 2020 roster, a decision that was overturned seven months later after some quick and desperate maneuvering by UWW. UWW replaced its president and announced stiff new anti-doping policies and new rule changes to speed up the action on the mat to make the sport more exciting to the casual spectator. Equalizing the weight classes among genders and adding a woman to its governing board were also key elements incorporated by UWW that gave the IOC reason to reverse its decision.

Wrestling was only given provisional status in the reversal, however, meaning that after the 2024 Olympics, the sport will once again have to go before the IOC and justify its place on the Olympic roster. The UWW has heeded this wake-up call and is prepared to show the world why this centuries-old sport is still relevant in today's world.

TEXT-DEPENDENT QUESTIONS:

1. In ancient Greece, citizens believed the gods of Olympus solved conflicts by doing what?

2. What is the variation of freestyle wrestling practiced at the middle and high school levels in the United States?

3. Who is the current star of American freestyle wrestling?

RESEARCH PROJECT:

Helen Maroulis is the first American woman to win a gold medal in wrestling. Look up how other American women have done in Olympic wrestling competition, and choose three athletes to write a report on. Be sure to include where they come from, how they got into the sport, how they came to national prominence, and their Olympic results.

SERIES GLOSSARY OF KEY TERMS

Acute Injury: Usually the result of a specific impact or traumatic event that occurs in one specific area of the body, such as a muscle, bone, or joint.

Calories: units of heat used to indicate the amount of energy that foods will produce in the human body.

Carbohydrates: substances found in certain foods (such as bread, rice, and potatoes) that provide the body with heat and energy and are made of carbon, hydrogen, and oxygen.

Cardiovascular: of or relating to the heart and blood vessels.

Concussion: a stunning, damaging, or shattering effect from a hard blow—especially a jarring injury of the brain resulting in a disturbance of cerebral function.

Confidence: faith in oneself and one's abilities without any suggestion of conceit or arrogance.

Cooldown: easy exercise, done after more intense activity, to allow the body to gradually transition to a resting or near-resting state.

Dietary Supplements: products taken orally that contain one or more ingredient (such as vitamins or amino acids) that are intended to supplement one's diet and are not considered food.

Dynamic: having active strength of body or mind.

Electrolytes: substances (such as sodium or calcium) that are ions in the body regulating the flow of nutrients into and waste products out of cells.

Flexible: applies to something that can be readily bent, twisted, or folded without any sign of injury.

Hamstrings: any of three muscles at the back of the thigh that function to flex and rotate the leg and extend the thigh.

Hydration: to supply with ample fluid or moisture.

Imagery: mental images, the products of imagination.

Mind-Set: a mental attitude or inclination.

Overuse Injury: an injury that is most likely to occur to the ankles, knees, hands, and wrists, due to the excessive use of these body parts during exercise and athletics.

Plyometrics: also known as "jump training" or "plyos," exercises in which muscles exert maximum force in short intervals of time, with the goal of increasing power (speed and strength).

Positive Mental Attitude (PMA): the philosophy that having an optimistic disposition in every situation in one's life attracts positive changes and increases achievement.

Protein: a nutrient found in food (as in meat, milk, eggs, and beans) that is made up of many amino acids joined together, is a necessary part of the diet, and is essential for normal cell structure and function.

Quadriceps: the greater extensor muscle of the front of the thigh that is divided into four parts.

Recovery: the act or process of becoming healthy after an illness or injury.

Resistance: relating to exercise, involving pushing against a source of resistance (such as a weight) to increase strength. Strength training, or resistance exercises, are those that build muscle. They create stronger and larger muscles by producing more and tougher muscle fibers to cope with the increasing weight demands.

Strategy: a careful plan or method.

Stretching: to extend one's body or limbs from a cramped, stooping, or relaxed position.

Tactics: actions or methods that are planned and used to achieve a particular goal.

Tendon: a tough piece of tissue in the body that connects a muscle to a bone.

Training: the process by which an athlete prepares for competition by exercising, practicing, and so on.

Warm-Up: exercise or practice especially before a game or contest—broadly, to get ready.

Workout: a practice or exercise to test or improve one's fitness for athletic competition, ability, or performance.

FURTHER READING:

Luke, Andrew. *Wrestling (Inside the World of Sports)*. Broomall, PA: Mason Crest, 2017.

Gable, Dan and Schulte, Scott. *A Wrestling Life: The Inspiring Stories of Dan Gable*. Iowa: University of Iowa Press, 2015.

Brandon, Leigh. *Anatomy of Sports Injuries: for Fitness and Rehabilitation*. London, UK: New Holland Publishers, 2013.

INTERNET RESOURCES:

United World Wrestling: *https://unitedworldwrestling.org/*

Sports Reference: *http://www.sports-reference.com/olympics/sports/WRE/*

FDA: Dietary Supplements
http://www.fda.gov/Food/DietarySupplements/default.htm

VIDEO CREDITS:

Check out Olympic champion Helen Maroulis's healthy weight loss regimen: *http://x-qr.net/1H7Z*

Virginia Cavalier Wrestling Club President Jim Harshaw talks about self-discipline: *http://x-qr.net/1Hea*

Check out World and Olympic champion Jordan Burroughs' intense training routine: *http://x-qr.net/1HH3*

Check out the nutrition plan for wrestlers at Division I University of Wisconsin: *http://x-qr.net/1GaA*

Watch American Kyle Snyder win the gold in Rio: *http://x-qr.net/1HLW*

PICTURE CREDITS

QR CODES AND LINKS TO THIRD-PARTY CONTENT

INDEX

In this index, page numbers in ***bold italics*** font indicate photos or videos.

Olympic wrestling, 62, 68–70, **68**, **69**, **70**
  See also specific athletes
overtraining, 32
overuse injuries, 32, 34

pain tolerance, 22
pinning, **28**, 64
Plato, 62, **62**
positive attitude, 15
proteins, 10, 55

running, **14**, 38

Sadulaev, Abdulrashid, 67
Sanderson, Cael, 8, 66–67
scholastic wrestling, 64–65
self-control, 19–20
self-discipline, 20–22, **21**
shoes, 26
singlets, 24, **24**, **25**, 26
sleep, 7–9
Smith, John, 66, 67
Snyder, Kyle, 12, 16, 67, **68**
sports drinks, 10–11, 57
sports psychologists, 16

Steiber, Logan, 12
strength training, 39–40, **41**, 42–43, **42**, **43**
stretching, 11–13, 34–35, **35**, 37
sumo wrestling, 63–64, **63**

Taylor, David, 7
toughness development, 22–23
training routines, 20, **38**

  See also endurance training; mental training; strength training
twisting or wrenching injuries, 32

Ungerleider, Steven, 15
uniforms, 24, **24**, **25**, 26
United World Wrestling (UWW), 70

Vlasov, Roman, **67**, 68
warm-up routines, 13–14
water

ABOUT THE AUTHOR

Peter Douglas is a former journalist, reporting on both sports and general news for many years at television stations in various locations across the US affiliated with NBC, CBS and Fox. Prior to his journalism career he worked with the Boston Red Sox Major League baseball team. An avid writer and sports enthusiast, he has authored 16 additional books on sports topics. In his downtime Peter enjoys family time with his wife and two young children and attending hockey and baseball games in his home city.